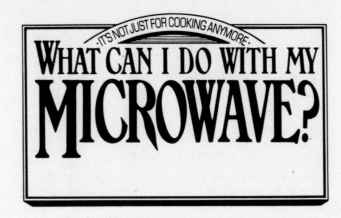

·IT'S NOT JUST FOR COOKING ANYMORE·

WHAT CAN I DO WITH MY MICROWAVE?

QUANTITY SALES

Most Dell books are available at special quantity discounts when purchased in bulk by corporations, organizations, and special-interest groups. Custom imprinting or excerpting can also be done to fit special needs. For details write: Dell Publishing, 666 Fifth Avenue, New York, NY 10103. Attn.: Special Sales Department.

INDIVIDUAL SALES

Are there any Dell books you want but cannot find in your local stores? If so, you can order them directly from us. You can get any Dell book in print. Simply include the book's title, author, and ISBN number if you have it, along with a check or money order (no cash can be accepted) for the full retail price plus $2.00 to cover shipping and handling. Mail to: Dell Readers Service, P.O. Box 5057, Des Plaines, IL 60017.

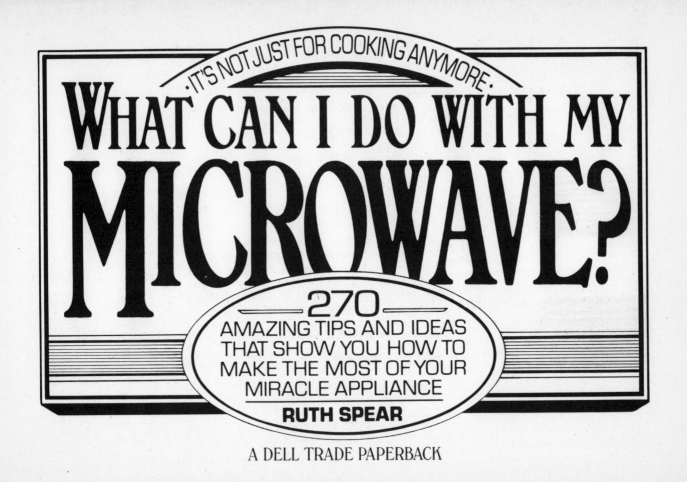

·IT'S NOT JUST FOR COOKING ANYMORE·

WHAT CAN I DO WITH MY MICROWAVE?

270
AMAZING TIPS AND IDEAS THAT SHOW YOU HOW TO MAKE THE MOST OF YOUR MIRACLE APPLIANCE

RUTH SPEAR

A DELL TRADE PAPERBACK

A DELL TRADE PAPERBACK
Published by
Dell Publishing
a division of
The Bantam Doubleday Dell Publishing Group, Inc.
666 Fifth Avenue
New York, New York 10103

ISBN: 0-440-50085-0

Printed in the United States of America
Published simultaneously in Canada
November 1988
10 9 8 7 6 5 4
S

CONTENTS

INTRODUCTION	8
MICROWAVE BASICS	11
How the Microwave Cooks	12
How to Cook in the Microwave	15
Dos and Don'ts	17
To Cover or Not to Cover	21
Converting and Adapting Recipes	22
EQUIPMENT	27
DEFROSTING AND FREEZING	33
BAKING	41
FOODS (A TO Z)	49
SNACKS	83
TIPS	87
INDEX	90

Note the following:

Times given are for a 650-watt oven. For small ovens, increase time according to the manufacturer's instruction booklet that accompanies all microwave ovens. If an item does not specify the type of cooking dish, assume it should always be microwave-safe. The same holds true for plastic wrap and plastic containers. And "tightly covered with plastic wrap" assumes you are going to vent the wrap, even if not specified.

For Harvey

INTRODUCTION

At last count, 54 million microwave ovens had been purchased in this country. My guess is that there are almost as many millions of people out there who have thought, said, or even screamed, "What can I do with this thing?" Relax. Here are the tips and ideas that will turn you into a confident, seasoned microwave user, endlessly delighting in the way this wonderful machine simplifies so many cooking chores.

Even, perhaps *especially*, knowledgeable cooks greatly resist the idea of changing everything they have learned, though the microwave's advantages in time savings and ease of preparation are apparent. This book will help you absorb those advantageous changes into your cooking lifestyle by helping you ease into modifying and enhancing, rather than drastically changing, the way you prepare food. There are many ways the microwave oven can make life easier, as well as ways it can't, and lots of tricks to learn to elevate its usefulness beyond the level of reheating coffee.

The way one uses this fabulous oven is very personal. No doubt some of the ideas in this book will suggest still other applications that are peculiar to your own cooking. For example, the true talent of the microwave lies in the areas of poaching, steaming, and braising, so any foods in your repertoire that rely on these moist methods should be examined for their microwave adaptability. On the other hand, I personally would never attempt to roast anything in the microwave, because the conventional oven does it so much better. Other things the microwave permits you to do handily, like making risottos without stirring, don't interest me either, because I not only love risottos but also love the ritual of cooking them. The microwave method, though easier, would actually deprive me of pleasure!

As with all sophisticated electronic equipment, there are dos and don'ts to observe. Familiarize yourself with them. You will be more likely to make creative use of your oven if you feel knowledgeable and secure in its use. And make sure anyone else who will be using the oven—children, household help, and others—knows the rules, too. Do take the time to read the manufacturer's booklet that accompanies your oven; these manuals are generally very well done, and even though there may not be a specific reference to the food you want to cook at the moment, all the basic information you need to start using your oven is there.

After you feel comfortable with the basic microwave principles, which are, after all, quite simple to master, allow yourself to be creative. That does not mean slavishly following new recipes—unless they really appeal—but rather letting the microwave do specific tasks in which it excels that are part of the recipes you and your family love. Where you go from there is up to you. Once your microwave becomes part of your food preparation scheme (which will happen more quickly than you could imagine possible) you'll wonder how you ever got along without it!

MICROWAVE BASICS

270 AMAZING TIPS & IDEAS

MICROWAVE BASICS

HOW THE MICROWAVE COOKS

1 Microwaves cook from the outside in, just as conventional ovens do. Microwave cooking is faster because the microwave itself doesn't have to heat the food to begin cooking it. Microwave energy penetrates food to a depth of somewhere between ¾ inch and 1½ inches vibrating the food molecules and thus causing heat. The heat then spreads to the center through the process of conduction, or heat transfer, as in conventional cooking.

2 Though microwave-safe dishes don't get hot in the microwave, they do become hot from contact with hot food, so have pot holders handy to avoid nasty surprises.

3 Because the food molecules are still vibrating and producing heat, microwaved foods continue to cook or heat after they are out of the oven and therefore must stand before being eaten. Small items with low density need only a few minutes of standing time; dense foods like turkey and potatoes can take 10 to 15 minutes. Also remember to be very careful before you bite into something with melted cheese, cornstarch-thickened fruit filled pastries, and the like.

4 Food left in the microwave after it has turned itself off will not burn, though it may cool off. The heat is in the food, not the oven.

5 The lower power levels of your microwave work by cycling the energy on and off, thus equalizing the heat in foods. When the heat is off, conduction takes over, spreading the heat gently from warm to cool areas, making these levels ideal for sensitive foods that might overheat or burn. Use them when in doubt.

6 When estimating cooking times, slightly undercook food and let it finish during standing time, which can range from 2 to 10 minutes. It can make the difference between food that is tender and food that is hard and overcooked. Undercooking is especially useful for fish.

7 In general food will not take on an attractive surface color in the microwave, as it does in conventional cooking, because the heat is no more intense on the outside or top of the food than on the inside. Depending on the food, first brown it conventionally by running it under the broiler or use a special microwave browning pan.

8 Moisture is driven to the surface during microwaving, which is why surfaces do not become crisp as in conventional cooking and why bread will become rock-hard if heated too long.

9 Fat is also drawn to the surface, which is part of what causes browning of meat in conventional cooking. As meat is rarely microwaved long enough for this to happen, only a very high-fat meat such as bacon will brown and/or crisp.

10 In a microwave, the food nearest the outside of the dish cooks most rapidly. Remember this when arranging food in a cooking dish—place the thickest parts of the food toward the outside.

11 The relationship of food to be cooked to the size dish you use can affect cooking time and the success of a recipe. If no instructions are given, select dishes that *just* hold the food and that have some depth so any liquid does not accidentally boil over.

HOW TO COOK IN THE MICROWAVE

12 The length of time required to cook food in the microwave depends on several factors, including volume. An increase in cooking time is not necessarily proportional to an increase in volume; two potatoes require more time than one, but not twice as much time.

13 A must for even cooking of meat and vegetables is uniform cut, size, and shape.

14 When cooking a combination of foods, such as carrots and cauliflower, place the longer-cooking items (the carrots) around the perimeter.

15 Bones and fat can cause irregular cooking. Large amounts of fat, such as found in a rib roast, absorb microwave energy, causing the immediately adjacent meat to be overcooked.

16 To facilitate fat removal, lay something absorbent like a slice of bread where the fat collects, instead of trying to spoon it out. Remove and discard as soon as the grease is absorbed.

17 Nonstick sprays don't work on browning pans—they don't spread properly in the microwave and will just burn where they land.

18 To reheat a dinner plate of food, place the thicker items at the perimeter, cover with a paper towel, and heat until the bottom of the plate is warm. The food will then be hot.

19 Liquids heated in the microwave can erupt if not mixed with air. When boiling water for tea, instant coffee, instant soups, etc., or when scalding or steaming milk, stir the liquid first.

20 Though a liquid heated in the microwave may not appear to be boiling, it may in fact erupt when you move the container, presenting a potential burn hazard. To be safe, let hot liquids sit untouched in the oven for 1 minute after the cooking time is completed, then gently stir with a spoon before moving.

21 Milk boils higher in the microwave than it does conventionally, so place in a glass measure larger than you would ordinarily select and watch it carefully. For more than a cup, remember to stir halfway though the heating time. This also applies to cooking or reheating soups that contain cream or milk.

22 If you must roast meat in the microwave, set it on a roasting rack placed in a casserole or baking dish, so fat extracted by the microwave can accumulate beneath and be discarded.

23 Microwave ovens, especially older ones, can have unevenly heated spots. If your oven is old and doesn't have an automatic turntable, you must remember to turn or reposition food that burns easily.

DOS AND DON'TS

24 *Do not* use metal in the microwave. This includes plates, dishes, skewers, plates with metallic trim, and containers with metal parts that may cause dangerous arcing (blue sparks). An exception: small, perfectly flat pieces of aluminum foil, used for shielding as explained in item 85.

MICROWAVE BASICS

25 *Do not* use wire twists to close cooking bags. They can act as antennae and cause arcing (blue sparks) or ignite and damage your oven. (See item 83.)

26 *Do not* place in the microwave food that comes in foil-lined containers, like a foil-lined milk carton. An exception: Frozen foods in metal containers *less than ¾ inch deep* may be heated in the container. Note that food may not heat evenly. It is better to remove the food from the tray and place it in a similar-sized container.

27 *Do not* boil eggs in their shell in the microwave. Built-up pressure will cause the eggs to explode. Peeled whole hard-boiled eggs *cannot* be reheated in the microwave for the same reason.

28 *Do not* attempt to deep-fat fry in your microwave.

29 *Do not* make popcorn in the microwave unless in a special microwave popper package.

30 *Do not* use in the microwave ceramic mugs or cups whose handles have been glued on. Handles may fall off with continued heating.

31 *Do not* use delicate glassware; use only heat-resistant glass cookware.

32 *Do not* try to sterilize canning jars in the microwave.

33 *Do not* use paper towels or cloths containing a synthetic fiber like nylon, which may cause paper or cloth to ignite.

34 *Do not* cook in plastic food storage bags, which are *not heat resistant* and may melt. Use cooking bags designated "microwave safe" (they may also be used for boiling and freezing).

35 *Do not* use conventional mercury-type candy or meat thermometers when heating food in the microwave. Special microwave thermometers are available.

36 *Do not* use paper towels or wax paper to reduce spatters when using the browning pan; the heat generated by the dish could cause them to catch fire.

37 *Do not* use salt in any form (including garlic salt, onion salt, etc.) on the surface of food to be microwaved; it leaves unattractive little dry spots. Don't add it to vegetable cooking water, either, as it can draw water from vegetables, wrinkling them. Either combine the salt with a sauce or salt food *after* exposure.

38 *Do not* use your microwave for big food loads. Big turkeys and lots of baked potatoes, for example, do better in your regular oven.

39 *Do not* heat fried frozen foods with a batter or crumb coating in the microwave; they will not be crisp.

40 *Prick* with a fork the skin of foods with nonporous skin *before* cooking in the microwave. Examples of foods with nonporous skins are apples, eggplant, and whole acorn and other hard-skinned winter squashes.

41 *Prick* the membrane of egg yolks before cooking as they are non-porous. Pierce several times lightly but firmly with a toothpick.

42 *Prick* sausage links with a fork and *score* frankfurters several times before cooking, to prevent bursting.

TO COVER OR NOT TO COVER

43 Use microwave-safe plastic wrap (vented) or a microwave-safe lid to cook foods that require steam to become tender.

44 Venting plastic wrap eliminates the possibility of the plastic melting on your food and also prevents steam buildups that could burn you when you remove the wrap. To vent, cover the dish tightly, then pull back one corner of the wrap.

45 Foods needing a lot of steam to cook well (such as vegetables with no added liquid), require a really tight cover. Place plastic wrap *between* the lid and the dish.

46 For food that does not need steam to become tender, like braised veal chops, use wax paper where conventionally you would cook a food by partially covering it to keep it from spattering.

47 To prevent spattering of food that normally is cooked uncovered, like bacon, use paper napkins or a paper towel as a covering.

48 Use paper napkins or a paper towel as a wrapping to keep the surfaces of bread and rolls dry when defrosting or heating them.

49 Use paper towels to absorb moisture that will be trapped between the food and the floor of the oven and make the bottom of the food undesirably soggy, such as when defrosting and heating coffeecake.

CONVERTING AND ADAPTING RECIPES

50 To adapt recipes for the microwave, it is helpful to find a microwave recipe that uses similar techniques as well as weight, bulk, and amount of ingredients and use it as a starting point.

51 When converting a regular recipe for use in the microwave, reduce the liquid requirement to two thirds and add more liquid, if you think you need it, during cooking. There is less evaporation than in conventional cooking.

52 To adapt a favorite conventional stir-fry recipe, make only half as much sauce as the recipe calls for.

53 Stir-fry recipes require less oil and soy sauce than when made in a wok. Stir-fry meat in a browning pan, prepare and heat through the sauce, add the vegetables, cover with microwave-safe plastic and vent, and shake the dish once as the vegetables cook. Add the reserved meat when the vegetables are crisp-tender, which can be as soon as 30 seconds.

54 Use a glass pie plate, soufflé dish, or casserole for stir-fry recipes.

55 To *double* an existing recipe, double all the ingredients but increase the liquid by one half the original amount and increase the time by one half to two thirds.

56 To *halve* an existing recipe, use half the ingredients and reduce the cooking time by half.

57 For good results, change the dish size and cooking time when you double or halve a microwave recipe; the idea is to have the food neither spread too thin in the dish (it may overcook or burn) or filled so high that it may spill over.

58 Microwave sauces made with cream at MEDIUM-HIGH and stir frequently to prevent boiling over.

59 Sauces you would normally make in a double boiler, like Hollandaise and Béarnaise, should be cooked at MEDIUM.

60 To microwave a flour-based sauce, cook the flour and fat together for a few minutes to develop color. Remove, blend in liquid with a wire whisk, return to the oven, and microwave until thickened, stirring occasionally. The power level depends on the type of liquid; use a higher level for broth, a lower level for milk-based sauces.

61 When microwaving a regular recipe, be sure to stir or rearrange the food and, if you have no turntable, rotate the dish at least once during cooking.

62 It is not worthwhile to cook regular rice in the microwave; the time required is virtually the same as for conventional cooking.

63 Herbs and spices can behave differently in microwave cooking. Generally, if your regular recipe calls for dried herbs, slightly decrease the amount when adapting the recipe for the microwave. If fresh herbs are to be used, add them later in the cooking or increase the amount as they can lose their punch.

64 Ground cinnamon, nutmeg, and ginger and dry mustard should be reduced in quantity.

65 Cumin, coriander, cardamom, and allspice should be increased in quantity.

66 Black pepper and white pepper increase in pungency and strength, so add them to taste after cooking or halve the amount you normally use.

67 Garlic loses its punch in the microwave. Either add it to a recipe toward the end of the cooking time or at least triple the quantity called for.

68 Liquor in recipes should be increased by one half the amount required in the original recipe if microwave cooking time is short and doubled for a dish to be microwaved more than 8 minutes.

69 *Glass measuring cups:* Cook in these rather than the plastic ones; it's easier to see what's happening with a liquid, and plastic may discolor with repeated microwave use.

70 For even heating, *round dishes* work best in the microwave.

71 Where possible, cook in microwave-safe plastic wrap or microwave-safe plastic bags (appropriately sealed and slit) to reduce cleanup.

72 No plastic bag the right size? Create your own: place food to be cooked on a big square of microwave-safe plastic wrap, bring up the edges in a butcher's fold, and tuck underneath.

73 *Foldable rack:* If your oven did not come with one, it's worth investing in. A foldable rack allows you to cook or reheat two dishes of food at the same time. Remember to increase the cooking time appropriately.

74 To test a *nonplastic* container for safety in the microwave, follow this procedure: Fill a glass measuring cup with water. Place in the microwave along with the container or plate you are testing. Heat 1 minute at HIGH. If the container is microwave-safe, it will be comfortably cool. *If the container is hot, do not use it in the microwave.* (The water in the cup will be hot either way.)

75 Improvise a meat-roasting rack by balancing meat to be defrosted or cooked on two ovenproof glass custard cups or an inverted microwave-safe bowl set in a casserole or baking dish. This allows the microwaves to get around the meat for even cooking.

76 When buying containers to cook in, consider a variety of sizes of glass or porcelain soufflé dishes that fit your oven. They are endlessly useful, can go right to the table, and go with everything.

77 Browning pans, whose specially coated surface reaches very high temperatures and mimicks the process by which a frying pan browns foods by immediately searing food placed on it, seem to work best with small, flat portions of meat such as hamburgers, small steaks, and chops.

78 When instructions call for a tight seal, do not rely on plastic box or bowl covers. Many microwave-safe bowls and dishes on the market come with plastic covers that are *not* microwave-safe. Use microwave-safe plastic wrap, vent as directed, and save the tops for refrigerator storage use.

79 Porcelain and pottery serving dishes can be used to cook in and serve as well. (See item 74.)

80 Keep plain white paper plates, towels, and napkins on hand for microwaving where indicated.

81 Wicker baskets may be used in the microwave (to heat finger towels, for example; see item 265), but be sure they are not constructed with metal staples.

82 Look for ovenproof paper dishes for your microwave; they come in appropriate shapes and sizes for baking and are also freezer-proof, so you can cook in them, freeze, then reheat and serve.

83 *Closing microwave bags:* The square plastic closures that come on loaves of bread are perfect for this.

84 *Stirring:* When a plastic-wrapped dish requires stirring, the easiest thing to do is remove it from the oven, remove the paper, stir, and replace the paper or put on a new piece.

85 *Shielding:* Though aluminum foil, being metal, should not be used because it reflects energy away from food, small pieces can be used to shield particular areas and slow or stop the cooking, thus preventing overcooking of those areas. Place the foil on parts of food being cooked or defrosted that are thinner than other parts, such as ends of roasts, tail sections of whole fish, wing tips of poultry—any part that is likely to cook before the rest of the food is finished. Make sure the foil is as *flat* as possible, with no folds or crimps, to prevent arcing.

270 AMAZING

DEFROSTING AND FREEZING

TIPS & IDEAS

DEFROSTING AND FREEZING

DEFROSTING

The quick defrosting of food is one of the primary delights of owning a microwave oven. It makes possible undreamed-of flexibility in meal planning. As long as you have the foods basic to your eating style in the freezer, you can make spur-of-the-moment meal decisions, defrost extra food if company appears, or rustle up a meal if plans change suddenly. A word on defrost times: Aside from packaged convenience foods, no two frozen foods are exactly alike, and all the books and charts in the world can only hope to approximate the information you need. If you cannot find a defrost time for the specific kind and weight of food you wish to defrost, look for something similar. Always use minimum times, check food frequently if you're not sure of the defrost time, and stir or turn it over if appropriate to redistribute exposed surfaces. It is better to set the timer for a second or third go-around than overdo the heat. With some foods, such as baked goods and breads, even a few seconds of extra heat can produce a disaster.

Make note of times and power levels that work for you until you evolve your own personal time chart for the foods you use most; keep it handy by posting it on the inside of a kitchen cabinet door.

86 If applicable, break food apart during defrosting time and remove the defrosted portions from the oven so they do not actually begin to cook while the balance is defrosting. This applies to ground beef, pork, or veal, as well as other foods in pieces.

87 If several items that need to be separated, such as fish fillets, are frozen together, turn over halfway through the defrost time and rinse under cold water to separate.

88 Turn over roasts, steaks, chops, Cornish hens, and spareribs halfway through the defrost time. Dense items like turkey breast, roasts, and whole chickens need to be turned two or three times.

89 If your oven has no DEFROST cycle: heat food at MEDIUM-LOW for short 4-minute periods or use the time suggested in your microwave booklet, then let stand 5 minutes. Repeat as needed. This method is preferable to using one long period of time, in which you run the risk that the defrosted outer edges of the food will begin to cook while the inside is still frozen.

90 After completely defrosting and before proceeding with cooking, rinse all poultry under cold water to remove any bacteria contamination frequently found on poultry skin.

91 If defrosting meat in a supermarket plastic tray or polystyrene plate, remove the tray or plate first. Microwaves will be attracted to any liquid that has accumulated on the tray, thus steaming the bottom of the meat while the rest is still frozen.

92 Loosely cover meat being defrosted with a sheet of wax paper to keep it from drying out.

93 At the halfway point, note whether any part of the defrosting meat feels warm. If so, shield it (see item 85) for the remaining defrost time.

94 When defrosting liver, drain liquid as it accumulates.

95 When defrosting a paper-wrapped package of frozen food, such as meat, remove the wrapping as soon as possible and replace with microwave-safe plastic wrap, which will hold in the heat and speed thawing.

96 To defrost 8- or 12-ounce cans of frozen fruit juice concentrate, remove the lid, and if the container is foil-lined, remove the contents as well and place in a glass measure, then defrost on MEDIUM-LOW 2½ to 5 minutes, depending on size.

97 Frozen pancake batter may be defrosted in the carton for 8 to 10 minutes. Shake vigorously twice during the defrost time. Do the same with your own homemade pancake mix, which you can make in quantity when you have time and freeze in washed-out cream or pint milk containers.

98 Frozen foods in foil containers deeper than ¾ inch must be removed from the container and placed in a microwave-safe container of appropriate size. Heat covered with microwave-safe plastic wrap or a tight-fitting lid.

99 Running hot water on the bottom of the closed package helps loosen hard-to-remove foods from their container.

100 For foods frozen in conventional plastic containers, run very hot water over the bottom and empty into a bowl or glass measure, and then defrost.

101 Though your oven may have a DEFROST cycle (usually 30% power), which is useful for dense items that take a relatively long time, like a roast, you can successfully defrost liquids more quickly, covered tightly, at full power, 100% or HIGH.

FREEZING

102 When freezing rolls, place them on a cookie sheet until just frozen. Wrap and seal, and then take out just the number you want.

103 Invest in microwave-safe plastic containers in which to freeze your staples, such as broths, tomato sauce, etc. To defrost, remove the lid and cover with microwave-safe plastic wrap.

104 To freeze stews for later microwave reheating, line the microwave container you will use with microwave-safe plastic wrap, fill with cooked food (leaving adequate head room), bring up the sides to cover, and put the container in the freezer. When frozen, remove from the container, label, date, and return to the freezer.

105 Freeze homemade chicken stock in 2-cup plastic containers to keep on hand for making delicious soups, sauces, rice pilafs, and risottos. Two cups will defrost at HIGH in 8 minutes or at DEFROST (30%) in 11 minutes.

106 When freezing anything with a liquid, make very sure the plastic container you use has no cracks in it; otherwise, when you defrost it you may find your oven floor awash.

107 For crisper textures, defrost coffee cakes, sweet rolls, and pizzas on microwave-safe trivets.

270 AMAZING

BAKING

TIPS & IDEAS

Baking pans

108 Grease round or square microwave-safe pans, then line with ungreased wax paper or paper toweling cut to size to absorb moisture and reduce the stickiness of the finished cake.

109 When baking from a conventional cake recipe in the microwave do *not* flour the cake pan. The flour will end up on the cake.

110 Round shapes microwave more evenly than squares or rectangles, whose corners may overcook as more energy penetrates these parts.

111 Ring shapes (Bundt pans and tube pans) yield more even cooking as they permit the microwaves to penetrate from all sides.

Cakes

112 Microwaved cakes not only cook in one third of the time of conventionally baked cakes; they also emerge unusually moist, lighter, and higher, because no crusty surface forms to retard rising.

113 Microwaved cakes do not brown and may be uneven, however, so stick to cakes that will be frosted.

114 As in conventional baking, cakes are done when they pull away from the sides of the pan.

115 If you are baking in the microwave and planning to serve the cake from the container you bake in, no greasing is necessary.

116 For best results, use cake recipes specifically formulated for the microwave.

117 Microwave cakes on a microwave-safe trivet to prevent soggy bottoms.

118 If a small area in the center of your cake appears to be undercooked and still moist when the sides test done, it will disappear upon standing. Do not test for doneness in those spots!

119 Microwaved cakes can be soft and sticky on top. To dry the top and make it easier to frost, sprinkle 1 teaspoon of graham cracker on each layer after baking.

120 Cakes and pastries rich in butter and sugar can be heated at MEDIUM for 30 to 60 seconds.

Cookies

121 Cookies baked in the microwave require 5 to 10 minutes of standing time; this will complete their cooking and firm them up. Set on a heat-resistant surface or wooden board.

Cupcakes

122 Use ovenproof glass custard cups, not regular muffin tins, when making cupcakes. Line each with two fluted paper cupcake liners—this helps produce more even, less sticky cupcakes.

123 Because they bake so quickly, holes can form in microwaved cupcakes. To prevent holes, cut through the unbaked batter several times with a toothpick or skewer when the batter is in the cupcake liners. This eliminates the air bubbles that cause holes.

124 Remove the cupcakes from the custard cups, leaving the paper liners *on*, to a rack to cool.

125 Sprinkle on dry toppings such as crushed nuts or streusel to dress up pale cupcake tops.

Pies

126 Open-faced pies should be cooked in the microwave only when the bottom crust has been precooked.

127 As pastry dough and fillings tend to cook unevenly, double-crust pies should not be cooked in the microwave.

128 Don't attempt a meringue topping in the microwave; it will not brown.

129 A whole pie will reheat at MEDIUM-HIGH in the microwave in 2 to 3 minutes, uncovered. Allow 2 to 3 minutes of standing time before cutting and serving.

130 Reheat filled pastries very carefully. Because sugar attracts microwaves, the sweet filling can still be very hot when the surface temperature of the pastry feels cool. The temperature will equalize during standing time.

Quick breads

131 Yeast-raised breads and crispy pastries do not do well in the microwave oven, so stick to quick breads.

132 Breads bake best in the microwave when formed into a ring.

133 Quick breads rise higher in the microwave, so don't fill baking dishes more than one-third to one-half full. If you have leftover batter, bake it as cupcakes.

134 If all of your ring baking pans are of metal, improvise one for microwaved bread making by shaping the dough into a ring in a glass pie plate and placing a lightly greased, narrow-based glass open side up in the center.

135 When baking in a traditional glass loaf pan, shield each end with 1½-inch strips of foil to prevent overcooking.

270 AMAZING

FOODS (A TO Z)

TIPS & IDEAS

FOODS (A to Z)

136 *To heat food:* As a general rule of thumb, for 1 cup of solid food, allow 2 minutes at HIGH.

137 *To bring food to room temperature:* Use your microwave to take the chill off refrigerated foods that are most flavorful at room temperature. For example, heat ½ pound of cheese, unwrapped, at MEDIUM for 45 seconds to 1 minute.

Almonds

138 To blanch almonds, microwave 1 cup of water to boiling, add the almonds, and microwave at HIGH for 30 seconds. Drain and skin.

139 To roast almonds or other nuts, place 1½ cups of nuts in a 9-inch pie plate and heat at HIGH for 4 to 5 minutes, stirring twice.

Artichokes

140 Two globe artichokes, trimmed as for conventional cooking will cook at HIGH in 10 minutes. Wrap individually in microwave-safe plastic wrap and let stand 5 minutes after removing from oven, before unwrapping.

Asparagus

141 Asparagus cooks beautifully in the microwave with no water. Scrape the stems, break off any woody portions, and arrange two to three deep, tips all pointing in the same direction, in a dish just large enough to hold them. Cover tightly with microwave-safe plastic wrap and cook; 1 pound will cook at HIGH in 4 minutes and 15 seconds and still be bright green. Two pounds will take 7 minutes. Unwrap them immediately as they can easily overcook. Run cold water over them to stop the cooking and set the color, then drain on paper toweling.

Avocados

142 To soften unripe avocados for guacamole, cut the avocado in half lengthwise, remove the pit, wrap each half tightly in microwave-safe plastic wrap, and place in the microwave at HIGH for 1 minute. Run immediately under cold water to stop the cooking and unwrap.

Babyfood

143 Puree cooked vegetables for baby and freeze in square-type ice cube trays. Defrost the cubes, bag them, and label. To use, place one cube in a custard cup and cook at HIGH for 45 to 60 seconds. Stir and check the temperature before feeding.

144 To heat 8 ounces of milk or formula to lukewarm, remove the cap and nipple, heat at MEDIUM for 45 to 60 seconds, replace and tighten the nipple, shake, and let stand 1 to 2 minutes. Test on your forearm. (Do *not* heat bottles with disposable linings in the microwave).

Bacon

145 Microwaved bacon shrinks less and doesn't curl or spatter, and cleanup is easy. Remember that bacon varies in thickness and the amounts of salt and sugar used in the curing, all of which will affect cooking time.

146 Separate cold bacon easily by heating unwrapped package at HIGH for 15 to 30 seconds.

147 Cook one to six slices of bacon at HIGH on a triple layer of paper toweling, directly on the oven floor, calculating 45 seconds to 1 minute per slice. Remove from the oven when the bacon is still slightly underdone and let stand 5 minutes after microwaving.

148 Several layers of bacon may be cooked at once with a paper towel between layers. Reduce the cooking time to 30 seconds per slice when making more than six slices.

Bagels

149 Bring a frozen bagel to eating softness by wrapping in a paper towel and heating at HIGH for 30 seconds. To warm or toast a bagel, use your toaster oven.

Bananas

150 To quick-ripen a too-hard banana for baby or for making banana bread, wrap 1 inch of each end of an underripe banana in a doubled, perfectly *smooth* piece of aluminum foil and microwave at HIGH for 60 seconds. Let cool before using.

Bread

151 To reheat 2 slices of bread or 2 small muffins or rolls at room temperature in the microwave, cover loosely in two layers of paper napkins or microwave-safe paper towels. Heat on HIGH for 15 to 20 seconds. If frozen, heat 35-45 seconds or until warm to the thumb. A loaf of Italian bread at room temperature takes 35-45 seconds.

270 AMAZING
TIPS & IDEAS

152 To restore stale French or Italian bread, wet one hand and sprinkle leftover bread just with the droplets that fall from your fingers. Wrap in microwave-safe plastic wrap and microwave at HIGH for 30 seconds. Remove, wrap in a paper napkin, and microwave at HIGH for 10 seconds. The bread will firm up on the outside as it cools and be freshly moist inside.

Broccoli

153 Cook 1 pound of broccoli florets in a dish just large enough to hold them in a single layer, covered tightly with microwave-safe plastic wrap, at HIGH for 4 minutes.

Brussels sprouts

154 Pierce an X in each stem end and place 1 pound in a 1½-quart casserole in a single layer with ¼ cup of water or chicken stock. Cover and microwave at HIGH for 4 to 8 minutes, depending on size. Let stand 3 minutes. Finish with a squeeze of lemon, salt, freshly ground pepper, and butter if you like.

Butter

155 To melt butter cut one stick (¼ pound) or less into pats, place in a glass cup or measure, cover the top with a paper napkin, and heat at HIGH for 2 minutes, keeping an eye on it.

156 To clarify butter in your microwave, cut ¼ pound (1 stick) into pats and heat at HIGH in a 2-cup glass measure, covered loosely with a paper towel, for 2 minutes. Skim the solids from the top, pour off the clear liquid (the clarified butter), and discard the milky solids at the bottom of the cup.

Cereal

157 Use a microwave-safe container large enough to prevent boiling over and, because microwaving heightens the boiling of milk-based foods, watch carefully. Heat cereal at LOW or MEDIUM-LOW and let stand for 1 to 2 minutes to complete the cooking. Cooking times for specific quantities will depend on the type of cereal. See item 207 for an example.

Cheese

158 Because fats heat very quickly in the microwave, a cheese topping can burn before the casserole it tops is cooked or heated through. Use a lower setting or add the topping halfway through the cooking time.

159 Mozzarella cheese can be exposed to microwaves only for as long as it takes to melt; after that it toughens. When making a dish that calls for this cheese as the top layer after the sauce, place it *under* the sauce instead.

Chestnuts

160 To peel chestnuts in the microwave, make a horizontal slash through the shell on the rounded side (without cutting through to the meat). Place in a 1-quart casserole with 1 cup of water, cover with microwave-safe plastic wrap or a glass lid, and cook at HIGH until the water boils, 2½ to 4 minutes. Let stand 5 to 10 minutes, then remove nuts one at a time and peel. Spread the peeled nuts on paper toweling to cool.

Chicken

161 To reheat chicken, wrap an individual piece of leftover cooked chicken in plastic and reheat at HIGH for 45 seconds to 1 minute and 15 seconds, depending on size. No dish, no cleanup.

162 Make many quick, satisfying dinners built around boned and skinned chicken breasts (recipes abound in microwave cookbooks). Keep at least half a dozen on hand, wrapped individually and frozen.

163 When you need chicken for salad, sandwiches, or hash, cook two skinned, boned, and split breasts (about 1 pound) in a glass pie plate, covered with microwave-safe plastic wrap, at HIGH for 5 minutes. On the bone, cook at HIGH for 7 to 8 minutes.

164 If you prefer dark meat, use two whole legs (thighs included), add ¼ cup broth, cover tightly, and microwave at HIGH for 7 minutes and 30 seconds.

165 When cooking a whole chicken, begin cooking breast side up, then turn breast down halfway through cooking time. Juices will run into the breast, keeping it moist, while legs and thighs finish cooking.

166 Cook a whole small chicken without the fatty skin and retain natural juiciness. Remove all skin with kitchen shears. Rub with a favorite mixture of spices (Indian or Mexican, for example) and microwave at HIGH in a deep casserole covered with wax paper for 18 minutes, half of this time breast side down. Let stand, covered, 15 minutes.

167 Cook chicken with no fat by steaming under vented microwave-safe plastic wrap with a little wine and herbs of your choice. This creates a natural sauce, which you can then cook down to concentrate flavor. Works well with fish too (see item 193).

168 To save time when barbecuing chicken halves or parts for a large group, microwave the chicken until almost done, then finish on the barbecue grill for color and charcoal flavor. The interior will be fully cooked and marvelously moist.

169 Freeze chicken livers covered with milk in a plastic container. (They get freezer burn easily.) Defrost, uncovered, at HIGH for 7 minutes for ½ pound, stirring once. Then use as desired.

Chocolate, melting

170 When melting chocolate, avoid HIGH, as you run the risk of scorching it. Heat ½ pound chocolate at MEDIUM or 50% power, which is easier to watch, for 3 to 4 minutes and stir after 2 minutes.

171 Always melt chocolate uncovered. No standing time is necessary.

172 Chocolate retains its shape when melted, which can be deceiving. Check by stirring frequently.

173 When melting chocolate together with some other ingredient, such as butter or cream, it is safe to use HIGH.

Clams

174 To open fresh clams, arrange a dozen rinsed and drained clams around the outer rim of a shallow baking dish or plate, cover, and microwave at HIGH for 2 to 4 minutes or just until clams start to open. Remove and return to the oven any that have not opened, heating for 1 minute. Discard any clams still not open. Remove the top shell of each clam with a clam knife.

175 When opening clams in the microwave, reserve any broth that exudes. Strain through a sieve lined with paper toweling or tissues and save to use in Bloody Marys, seafood risottos, and fish soups.

Coconut

176 To toast coconut, sprinkle ½ cup grated fresh coconut in a thin layer in a 9-inch pie plate. Microwave at MEDIUM-HIGH for 3 to 4 minutes, until light brown, tossing with a fork after each minute. Store in an airtight container.

Corn

177 To cook corn on the cob, pull back the husk, remove the silk, pull the husk back up into place, and secure with a rubber band. Cook, uncovered, in a single layer directly on the oven floor. One ear will cook at HIGH in 2 minutes, two ears in 5 minutes, six ears in 14 minutes.

178 For a spicy side dish, mix one 1-pound can corn kernels with one jalapeño pepper, seeded and diced, and ½ jarred pimiento, covered, at HIGH for 3 to 4 minutes.

Crabs

179 Instead of boiling live crabs, steam a dozen with packaged crab boil mix, covered tightly in a microwave-safe dish at HIGH for 15 minutes. For 2 dozen, cook for 25 minutes.

Cream cheese

180 To soften cream cheese for cheesecake, frostings, or other uses, microwave in a glass bowl at MEDIUM for 1 to 2 minutes.

Curry

181 Because they do not require browning the meat, chicken and lamb curries can be made with ease in the microwave. Use your regular recipe and reduce the liquid requirement (see item 51). Let stand 5 minutes before serving.

Desserts

182 Make a *quick dessert* by defrosting a 10-ounce package of frozen strawberries on HIGH in syrup for 1 minute and 45 seconds. Drain, add 2 tablespoons of sugar, and puree in a blender or food processor until the sugar has dissolved. Use over fresh peaches, blueberries, or ice cream.

183 Make quick *blueberry sauce* to use as an ice cream topping or to use up berries that have been around for several days: Microwave 1 pint picked-over blueberries with 2 or 3 tablespoons of sugar if you like, in a 4-cup measure covered with microwave-safe plastic wrap at HIGH for 3 minutes. Serve warm. Good with pancakes, too.

184 Make a quick *fruit gratin* with 1 pound of your favorite fruit, sliced (pears, for example), and ¾ cup apple juice. Microwave covered, at HIGH for 1 minute, pour off the liquid, and top with crushed gingersnaps or macaroons.

185 Combine the ingredients for your favorite *dried fruit compote* in a bowl, cover with microwave-safe plastic wrap, and cook at HIGH for 9 minutes. Stir three times. Remove, stir, and serve warm.

186 Make a good *dessert for dieters*: Microwave cored, whole fresh pears, covered, with a splash of wine, some spices, perhaps orange peel, in a dish at least 2 inches deep. One pear takes about 3 minutes at HIGH. You'll find the flavor concentrated without the use of sugar.

Dried fruits

187 To soften dried fruits, place fruit in a single layer on a plate, sprinkle with water, cover with microwave-safe plastic wrap, and heat at HIGH for 30 to 40 seconds. Raisins take about 1½ minutes and work best in a glass measuring cup.

Eggs

188 Refrigerated eggs can be brought to room temperature in the microwave in 8 to 10 seconds. (See also item 27.)

Eggplant

189 Here's a treat from the East: Prick 1 medium eggplant and microwave on a paper towel at HIGH for 5 to 7 minutes or until it collapses. Cool in the refrigerator for 30 minutes, scoop out flesh into a food processor, and add 3 tablespoons of oil plus lemon juice, soy sauce, garlic, a dash of sugar, and freshly ground pepper to taste. A handful of pine nuts is nice, too. Serve as a dip.

English muffins

190 English muffins that have already been toasted can be reheated handily. Place on paper toweling to absorb excess moisture from the steam trapped under them. Check after heating at HIGH for 15 seconds.

Fish

191 Even when you have specific cooking times for fish, use your eye and undercook slightly; fish continues to cook out of the oven.

192 This technique for poaching fish works beautifully in the microwave: Place room-temperature fish steaks, rolled fillets, or a small whole fish in a glass pie plate. Almost cover with poaching liquid, cover tightly with microwave-safe plastic wrap, and cook, allowing 8 minutes per pound.

193 To make fish sauce, boil down the liquid in which you have poached fish to concentrate the flavor. Place the liquid in a large glass measure and cook at HIGH until reduced to half its volume. Swirl in two pats of butter, season to taste, and use to sauce fish.

194 Fish stock for your freezer is easy in the microwave. Place all ingredients—head, bones, etc.—in an 8-cup glass measure, cover tightly with microwave-safe plastic wrap, cook at HIGH for 30 minutes, strain, and cool.

195 To dress up flounder, sole, or trout, heat 1 tablespoon of butter in a browning pan at HIGH for 1 minute and 30 seconds. Add 2 tablespoons of blanched sliced almonds and cook 1 minute longer, stirring once.

FOODS (A to Z)

Frozen entrees	**196**	To heat frozen entrees, place an 8- to 10-ounce pouch pack on a microwave-safe dish, slash the pouch, and cook at HIGH for 6 to 8 minutes.
Fudge, hot	**197**	To achieve a very good consistency, heat 1 cup of hot fudge topping in a ceramic or glass pitcher or heat the whole jar with the lid off at HIGH for 3 to 5 minutes, stirring once halfway through the heating time.
Gravy	**198**	Reheat gravy right in the gravyboat: 1 cup at room temperature will heat, covered, at HIGH in 2 minutes. If refrigerated, double the time.
Honey	**199**	Melt crystallized honey by removing the metal lid and placing the jar in microwave at HIGH for 30 to 45 seconds. For a large jar, repeat, then cool, cap, and store. Works for preserves that have crystallized, too.

Hors d'oeuvres

200 Plan hors d'oeuvres with your microwave in mind: Cocktail sausages, stuffed mushrooms, meatballs, etc., can be heated or cooked and served in the same container in seconds. Use a paper towel lining to absorb moisture and spatters.

Hot punch

201 If your oven has a temperature-hold setting, it is ideal to use for hot punches. Mulled wine and glögg can be held at 165 degrees without losing their kick.

Ice cream

202 To make ice cream scoopable, warm ½ gallon at LOW for 2 to 4 minutes and watch carefully. Or microwave it at HIGH for 30 seconds and let stand 2 minutes, then repeat, always watching for the moment of proper consistency.

Juice

203 You can get more juice from your citrus fruit if you prick lemons, limes, oranges, or grapefruits with a fork once or twice first, and then microwave at HIGH for 15 to 20 seconds per piece. Allow the fruit to stand 1 to 2 minutes, then roll between the palms of your hands before squeezing. When doing several at a time, place them in a circle on the floor of the oven.

Lemon or orange peel

204 Make your own dried lemon or orange peel when you are squeezing lemons or oranges for something else: Grate the peel, place in a glass bowl, and microwave at HIGH for 30 to 60 seconds or until dry, stirring once. Store in the refrigerator or freezer in a tightly sealed jar.

Meat loaf

205 Meat loaf will cook more quickly if it is shaped into a ring in a 9-inch glass pie plate.

Mussels

206 Scrubbed and debearded mussels may be cooked with or without liquid, depending on how they are to be used. Place hinge end down in a dish that keeps them snugly in standing position and cover tightly. Two pounds will cook at HIGH in 4 to 7 minutes. Stir after 3 minutes. If a liquid is added, add 1 minute.

Oatmeal

207 Make old-fashioned oatmeal in a jiffy: Combine ⅓ cup of rolled oats (not the quick-cooking variety) with ¾ cup of water in a 2-cup glass measure. Cook at HIGH for 2 minutes and 30 seconds; let stand 1 minute.

Onions

208 Try these for hamburgers: Slice two yellow or one Spanish onion, place in a microwave-safe dish with one pat of butter, and microwave at HIGH for 4 minutes, stirring twice.

209 To peel pearl onions or small white onions easily, blanch them by microwaving 1 pound (root ends trimmed) in a single layer with 2 tablespoons of water at HIGH for 2 minutes, uncovered. Let cool a bit before slipping off the skins.

Osso buco

210 Love osso buco? Four shanks will cook at HIGH in 16 minutes, covered tightly. Use your regular recipe, browning the shanks on top of the stove first.

Peas

211 To make frozen peas taste more like fresh, place the block icy side up in a microwave-safe dish with 2 tablespoons of chicken broth, 1 tablespoon of butter, and a pinch each of sugar and dried thyme. Cover and cook at HIGH for 4 minutes, stirring after 2 minutes. Let stand 3 minutes.

Pies

212 To reheat cold fruit pies or tarts, place on a plate and heat at HIGH for 45 seconds to 1½ minutes, depending on thickness.

Pine nuts

213 Toast ¼ cup of pine nuts in a single layer at HIGH for 2 to 3 minutes, until golden, stirring once halfway through the cooking time. Great addition to pasta, pilafs, and salads.

Pizza

214 To reheat pizza, microwave one or two slices on a paper plate or napkin at HIGH for 1 to 2 minutes. Let stand 1 to 2 minutes before eating.

Polenta

215 Make hassle-free polenta in your microwave. In a 3-quart casserole combine 1 cup of coarse yellow cornmeal with 3½ cups of water, 1 tablespoon of olive oil, and a dash of salt. Cover tightly and cook at HIGH for 9 to 12 minutes, stirring after 5 minutes. Watch closely. When all the water appears to be absorbed, stir again.

Pork chops

216 Cooking pork chops in the microwave long enough to achieve an appealing color can also toughen and dry them. Try this: Next time your outdoor grill is lit, devote some extra time to searing your favorite chops, then wrap, label, and freeze promptly. To use, defrost and microwave at HIGH for 60 to 90 seconds per chop, depending on thickness. That way you'll have both the color and the tenderness.

FOODS (A to Z)

Potato chips and crackers	**217** To recrisp them, arrange potato chips and crackers in a single layer on a paper plate or paper towel and microwave at HIGH for 45 seconds to 1½ minutes, depending on the amount.
Potato salad	**218** Cut the time required for your favorite potato salad by microwaving 3 pounds of peeled potatoes, cut into ¾-inch dice and sprinkled with ¼ cup of water, in a 3-quart casserole. Cook at HIGH for 12 minutes, stirring every 3 minutes. Then cool slightly, add other ingredients, cool completely, and refrigerate.
Potatoes, baked	**219** One medium potato will bake at HIGH in 3 to 5 minutes.
	220 When baking several potatoes, it helps to have them all the same size so they will finish together.
	221 Prick each well-scrubbed potato twice with a fork so that some of the steam can escape as they cook.

222 It is important to elevate the potato off the even floor so the microwaves can get to all sides. Use a microwave meat rack or even several chopsticks with a paper towel placed on top.

223 Place the fattest end of the potato toward the center; when cooking several, arrange them like the spokes of a wheel, at least an inch apart. Turn the potatoes over and reposition halfway through the cooking time so they will cook more evenly.

224 Remove the potatoes from the oven, wrap in aluminum foil, *shiny side in*, and cover with a casserole dish to allow them to finish cooking and hold in the heat. Let stand 5 to 10 minutes before serving.

Pretzels and popcorn

225 To refresh stale pretzels and popcorn, spread 2 cups on a paper plate and microwave at HIGH for 30 to 45 seconds. They will firm up as they cool.

Puddings and custards	**226** Puddings and custards are easy to make in the microwave as much of the stirring is eliminated. Use a conventional recipe and make in a 2-quart casserole.
Salads	**227** To make a main-course salad, core and coarsely shred one-half head of red cabbage (cut lengthwise), wrap in microwave-safe plastic wrap, and cook on a paper plate at HIGH for 2 minutes. Drain, rinse, and pat dry. Combine with sliced mushrooms, sliced sweet red pepper, and canned chick-peas and dress with vinaigrette.
Sauces	**228** Make savory sauces like Béchamel and Mornay in the microwave to prevent lumps from forming.
	229 Hollandaise is also fabulously easy, and there's no threat of curdling or separating. For Hollandaise and other recipes that call for eggs, be sure to stir often and check the consistency at 30-second intervals.

Sausage

230 Microwave sausage links or patties in a preheated browning pan. For four links, cook on HIGH for 25 to 35 seconds. Turn and cook for another 30 to 45 seconds. For four patties, cook for 1½ minutes on HIGH. Turn and cook for another 1½ to 2 minutes.

Scallops

231 Sea Scallops are a dieter's delight because they are without fat. Arrange ½ pound of sea scallops in a single layer in a shallow microwave-safe dish. Cover tightly with microwave-safe plastic wrap and cook at HIGH for 2 minutes. Season with salt, freshly ground pepper, and a squeeze of lemon.

Sesame seeds

232 To toast sesame seeds, place ¼ cup untoasted seeds in a small ovenproof glass bowl and cook at HIGH for 3 to 4 minutes, stirring twice. Let stand 2 to 3 minutes.

Shrimp

233 For a quick first course or main-course salad base, cook 1 pound of medium shrimp in the shell in a 2-quart microwave-safe dish, covered tightly with plastic wrap, at HIGH for 3 to 4 minutes. Shake the dish once to redistribute the shrimp.

234 To avoid overcooking (and toughening) shrimp, undercook them slightly and let them finish as they stand.

Snow peas

235 For a quick, pretty vegetable accompaniment, combine 4 ounces of fresh snow peas in a microwave-safe dish with 1 teaspoon of vegetable oil, a drop of dark sesame oil, and 1 teaspoon of sesame seeds. Toss to coat, spread out evenly in the dish, cover tightly, and cook at HIGH for 1 minute and 30 seconds. Salt lightly.

Soup

236 Reheat 1 cup of leftover soup in a 2-cup glass measure or bowl at HIGH for 2 minutes. Two cups in a quart measure will take 3 minutes.

Spareribs

237 To shorten barbecue cooking time, partially cook ribs on the roasting rack in the microwave and finish on the grill.

Squash

238 Cook two seeded acorn squash halves, wrapped tightly in microwave-safe plastic wrap, with 1 lump of butter and a grating of nutmeg or other favorite spice, at HIGH for 7 minutes. Season with salt and freshly ground pepper.

239 For an elegant vegetable accompaniment to meat or fish, cook squash as in item 238, but without flavoring, scoop out the flesh, and puree in a food processor with one peeled garlic clove and a knob of butter. Reheat the puree at HIGH for 1 minute, and season to taste.

240 Cook extra squash in the microwave, puree in a food processor and freeze to have on hand for elegant hearty squash soup (see any cookbook). One pound of squash will give you about 1 cup of puree, which will defrost at HIGH in 3 minutes and 30 seconds.

Stew

241 When making a favorite stew, double the recipe and freeze half for another meal, which you can defrost and reheat in record time. (See item 104.)

242 When adding dumplings to a stew in the microwave, make them small. They will puff up considerably more than in conventional cooking.

243 If some pieces of meat are tough in a microwaved stew, it could be that not all were covered equally with liquid; try to keep them uniformly submerged.

Sugar, brown

244 To soften brown sugar, place 1 cup (or the rough equivalent) of hard brown sugar in a glass dish with a slice of bread or a wedge of apple. Cover with microwave-safe plastic wrap and heat at HIGH for 30 to 60 seconds.

Syrup

245 Warm syrup for pancakes right in the pitcher you will serve it in. Depending on quantity, check after 30 seconds.

Tomatoes

246 To peel a tomato, put enough water to cover in a bowl or glass measure and microwave at HIGH until it boils, 2½ to 3 minutes. Drop in a tomato for a few seconds (no power), then peel in strips. Works for peaches, too.

Tortillas

247 To warm flour tortillas, wrap them, four at a time, in damp paper towels and heat at HIGH for 15 to 20 seconds.

Vegetables, general advice

248 Always stir cut-up vegetables to redistribute and reposition them halfway through their cooking time, as those in the center of the dish and oven cook more slowly.

249 If you don't want to be bothered with stirring, cook cut-up vegetables like sliced carrots, cauliflower, or broccoli florets in a microwave-safe tube pan.

250 If you like your vegetables lightly buttered, add the butter to the cooking water.

251 For quick vegetable fixings when you've been working all day, buy cleaned, raw, cut-up vegetables (either one kind or a mixture of several with similar cooking times) at a salad bar on your way home and microwave, wrapped in plastic.

252 To cook a small amount of vegetables, wrap them in a paper towel, hold the packet under running water, gently squeeze out the excess water, place the packet on a microwave-safe plate, and microwave.

Wild rice

253 Cook wild rice with very little fuss: Microwave 1 cup with 2 cups of water in an 8-cup measure, covered tightly with microwave-safe plastic wrap, at HIGH for 12 minutes. Uncover and let stand 15 minutes. Then add butter and seasonings as desired.

Zucchini

254 Remove the stem and blossom ends of 1 pound of scrubbed zucchini, slice into ½-inch rounds, and cook with 1 tablespoon of water, covered with microwave-safe plastic wrap, at HIGH for 3 minutes.

One of the jobs the microwave does best is to help you prepare extra-quick snacks with very little cleanup. Great for kids and adults!

Grilled cheese sandwich

255 Preheat a browning pan at HIGH. Place two slices of cheese between slices of bread, butter the *outside* of the sandwiches, flatten them lightly with a spatula, place in the preheated pan, and let stand outside the oven for 15 to 20 seconds. Repeat with side two, increasing the standing time slightly. If necessary, microwave at HIGH for 15 to 25 seconds more to finish melting the cheese.

Ham and cheese on a croissant

256 Spread each half of a split croissant with Dijon mustard and top with 1 slice of Swiss cheese and 1 slice of Westphalian or regular ham. Place on a paper towel, cover with another, and microwave at HIGH for 40 seconds.

Hot chocolate

257 According to package directions, mix cocoa powder, sugar, and milk in a 2-cup measure and microwave at HIGH for 2 to 2½ minutes, stirring once, until hot.

Hot dogs

258 *Dog in a bun:* An uncooked hot dog in a bun will cook at HIGH in 35 to 40 seconds. Be sure to wrap in a paper towel or napkin.

259 *Texas Tommy:* Place a pricked hot dog and a piece of American cheese in each of two buns, wrap in a paper towel or napkin, and cook at HIGH for 1 minute. Let stand 30 seconds.

Macaroni and cheese

260 Make this dish from your favorite recipe and freeze as in item 103 or 104. Defrost at HIGH for 3 minutes, unwrap, put in an ovenproof container, and run under the regular broiler until the top is brown and bubbly.

Mini-pizza

261 Place a split and toasted English muffin on a paper plate, spread with marinara sauce or other tomato sauce, and top with shredded mozzarella cheese, a sprinkle of dried oregano, pepperoni slices, and a pinch of hot pepper flakes if you like. Cook at MEDIUM for 1 to 2 minutes, until the cheese melts. Let stand 2 minutes before eating.

Nachos

262 Arrange taco chips on a microwave-safe dish or paper plate and top with any or all of canned refried beans, grated Jack or cheddar cheese, thinly sliced jalapeños, and salsa. Cook, uncovered, at HIGH for about 1 minute or until the cheese melts. Let stand 2 minutes before eating .

S'Mores

263 Kids love these and can make them easily . Place a graham cracker on a paper towel or plate and top with a piece of a plain chocolate bar or chocolate chips, then with a marshmallow. Microwave at HIGH for 15 to 30 seconds or until the marshmallow starts to expand like a cloud (the chocolate will appear not to have melted, but it will be. Wait a few seconds before eating.

270 AMAZING

TIPS

TIPS & IDEAS

Most manufacturers will tell you your microwave is strictly for cooking, and by and large I agree. Here, however, are a few hints you may find fun and useful.

Hot compress

264 To make a nondrippy compress, place a dampened washcloth in the microwave and warm at HIGH for 30 seconds or until pleasantly hot.

Hot towels

265 When serving spareribs, barbecued chicken, or any messy finger food, fragrant hot towels are a nice touch. Dampen thin white washcloths with water and a sprinkle of lemon juice and roll up. Stack side by side in a small, shallow wicker basket (without metal staples) and microwave at HIGH for 20 to 25 seconds. Serve with tongs and shake out if too hot.

Ironing linens

266 To make ironing tablecloths, napkins, and other linens easier, sprinkle lightly with water, place in a 1-gallon plastic garbage bag, and twist loosely to close. Microwave at HIGH for 1 minute or until the cloth is warm to the touch.

Kids and the microwave

267 Introduce kids to the microwave gradually; go over the ground rules, then let them start by defrosting bagels (item 149) and making hot dogs (item 258), mini-pizzas (item 261), and S'Mores (item 263).

Microwave odors

268 Combine the juice and peel of 1 lemon with enough water in a measure to make ½ cup liquid. Heat at HIGH for 5 minutes. Wipe the oven interior with a clean, damp cloth.

269 To remove lingering fish or bacon odors from your oven, bring 1 cup of water with 1 cup of vinegar to a boil in a glass measure in the microwave and let cool to lukewarm. Wipe the interior of the oven with a paper towel dipped in the liquid.

Buying a new microwave

270 If you are about to buy a microwave and are considering several models, take an 8-cup glass measure to the store and try to buy a microwave that will accommodate it. If you have the space, an 8-cup measure is invaluable in cooking and reheating all kinds of liquids.

INDEX

A

Almonds, 50
Aluminum foil, 17, 31, 73
Artichokes, 50
Asparagus, 51
Avocados, 51

B

Babyfood, 51-52
Bacon, 52-53
Bagels, 53
Baking, 42-47
Baking pans, 42, 46-47
Bananas, 53
Barbecuing, microwaving before, 58, 76
Blueberries, 62
Breads, 14, 53-54
  quick, 46-47
Broccoli, 54
Browning foods, 13, 14, 20, 29, 43, 45
Browning pans, 13, 20, 29, 65, 84
Brown sugar, 78
Brussels sprouts, 54

Butter, 55
Buying a new microwave, 89

C

Cakes, 39, 42-44
Cereal, 55, 69
Cheese, 56, 84
Chestnuts, 56
Chicken, 36, 57-59
Chicken livers, 59
Chocolate, 59, 85
Clams, 60
Coconut, 60
Compress, hot, 88
Cookies, 44, 86
Cooking times, estimating, 13, 15
Corn, 61
Covering or not covering foods, 21-22
Crabs, 61
Crackers, 72
Cream cheese, 61
Cupcakes, 44-45
Curry, 62
Custard, 74
Custard cups, 44, 45

D

Defrosting tips, 22, 34-38, 39
Desserts, 62-63
  see also Baking
Dishes, microwave-safe, 12, 17, 19, 28-30, 37
  for defrosting and freezing, 37-38
  size of, relative to food, 14, 24
  for stir-frying, 23
  testing, 29

E

Eggplant, 64
Eggs, 18, 21, 64
English muffins, 64, 86
Equipment, 28-31
  see also specific equipments, e.g.,
  Dishes, microwave-safe

F

Fat, 14, 15, 18
Fish, 64-65
  see also specific types of fish

Frankfurters, 21, 85

Frankfurters, 21, 85
Freezing tips, 30, 38-39
Frozen entrees, heating, 66
Fruits, 62-63
  see also individual fruits
Fudge, hot, 66

G

Gravy, 66
Grilled cheese sandwich, 84

H

Ham and cheese on a croissant, 84
Heating food, general rule for, 50
  see also specific foods
Herbs and spices, 25-26
Honey, 66
Hors d'oeuvres, 67
Hot dogs, 21, 85

I

Ice cream, 67
Ironing linens, 88

J

Juices, 37, 68

K

Kids and the microwave, 86

L

Large amounts of food, 20
Lemon peel, 68
Liquids, 16, 23, 36, 38, 39
Liquor, 26
Liver, 36

M

Macaroni and cheese, 85
Measuring cups, 28
Meat loaf, 68
Meats, 14, 15, 17, 29, 35
  see also specific types of meat
Metal, 17-18, 30

Microwave cooking:
  dos and don'ts of, 17-21
  explanation of, 12-17
Milk, 16-17, 52
Mussels, 69

N

Nachos, 86
Nonstick sprays, 16

O

Oatmeal, 69
Odors, microwave, 89
Onions, 69
Orange peel, 68
Osso buco, 70

P

Pancake batter, defrosting, 37
Paper plates and dishes, 30
Paper towels, 19, 20, 22, 30, 42

Pears, 63
Peas, 70
Pies, 45-46, 70
Pine nuts, 70
Pizza, 39, 71, 86
Plastic cooking bags, 19, 28, 31
Plastic wrap, 21, 28, 30, 37
Poaching fish, 65
Polenta, 71
Popcorn, 18, 73
Pork chops, 71
Potato(es), 20
    baked, 72-73
    salad, 72
Potato chips, 72
Poultry, 36, 57-59
Power levels, use of lower, 13, 24, 35, 44
Pretzels, 73
Pricking non-porous foods, 20-21
Pudding, 74
Punches, 67

Q

Quick breads, 46-47

R

Racks, 28, 29
Recipes, converting and adapting, 22-26
    see also specific foods
Reheating foods, 16, 45-46
    see also specific foods
Repositioning foods, 17, 25, 35
Rice, 25
    wild, 80
Rolls, freezing and defrosting, 38, 39
Room temperature, bringing food to, 50, 64

S

Salads, 72, 74
Salt, 20
Sauces, 24, 62, 65, 74
Sausages, 21, 75
Scallops, 75
Sesame seeds, 75
Shielding food, 31, 36, 47
Shrimp, 75-76
S'Mores, 86
Snacks, 84-86

Snow peas, 76
Soup, 76
Spareribs, 76
Spices, 25-26
Squash, 77, 81
Standing time for foods, 12, 13, 16, 43, 45, 73
Sterilizing, 19
Stews, 39, 77-78
Stir-frying, 23
Stirring, 31
Stock, 39, 65
Strawberries, 62
Sugar, brown, 78
Syrup, 78

T

Thermometers, 19
Tomatoes, 79
Tortillas, 79
Towels, hot, 88
Trivets, microwave-safe, 39, 43

U

Uniformity in cut of meat and vegetables, 15

V

Vegetables, 15, 21, 79-80
  see also specific vegetables

W

Wax paper, 22, 36, 42
Wicker baskets, 30
Wild rice, 80
Wire twists, 18

Z

Zucchini, 81

ABOUT THE AUTHOR

Ruth Spear is a journalist and food writer whose articles on food have appeared in *New York* magazine, *Cuisine*, *Food & Wine*, *Cosmopolitan*, and the Time-Life Cookbook series. Her food column has appeared frequently in the Sunday magazine section of the *New York Daily News*, and she was for many years the food editor of *Avenue* magazine. She is the author of *Cooking Fish and Shellfish* (Doubleday & Co.), *The East Hampton Cookbook* (Dell Publishing), and *The Classic Vegetable Cookbook* (Harper & Row).